OUR
HEALTH

STEWART ROSS

Wayland

Stewart Ross

STARTING HISTORY

Food We Ate
How We Travelled
Our Environment
Our Family
Our Health
Our Holidays
Our Schools
Shopping
What We Wore
Where We Lived

First published in 1992 by
Wayland (Publishers) Ltd
61 Western Road, Hove
East Sussex, BN3 1JD

© Copyright 1992 Wayland (Publishers) Ltd

Editor: Geraldine Purcell
Series Designer: Derek Lee

British Library Cataloguing in Publication Data

Ross, Stewart
Our Health.—(Starting History Series)
I. Title   II. Series
362.10941

ISBN 0-7502-0627-6

Typeset by Dorchester Typesetting Group Ltd
Printed and bound in Belgium by Casterman S.A.

PICTURE ACKNOWLEDGEMENTS

Eye Ubiquitous 11 (top), (P Blake) 16, (B Turner) 20; Hulton-Deutsch Collection 5, 9, 11 (bottom), 17, 18, 23 (bottom); Hulton-Radio Times Collection 6; The Mansell Collection 10, 22; Topham cover, 7 (bottom), 13, 14, 15, 19, 21, 25, 27, 29 (bottom); Wayland Picture Library 7 (top), 23 (top), 28, 29 (top); ZEFA 4, 8, 12, 24, 26.

Words that appear in **bold** are explained in the glossary on page 31.

Starting History is designed to be used as source material for Key Stage One of the National Curriculum. The main text and photographs reflect the requirements of AT1 (Understanding history in its setting) and AT3 (Acquiring and evaluating historical information). The personal accounts are intended to introduce different points of view (AT2 – Understanding points of view and interpretations) and suggestions for activities and further research (AT3 – Development of ability to acquire evidence from historical sources) can be found on page 31.

CONTENTS

HOW ARE YOU?

These children are enjoying themselves in the fresh air. What are they doing? Kite flying is great fun, because you get plenty of exercise.

These children are fit and healthy. We know much more than we used to about how to keep healthy.

Isn't this picture sad? It was taken a hundred years ago. The brother and sister had an illness called **rickets**. Many people used to get this **disease** because doctors did not understand what caused it.

Nowadays we can protect people from many diseases. This is one of the ways our health care has changed over the last seventy-five years.

Can you see the nurse in this picture? She is giving the little girl her medicine.

The nurse is working for the **National Health Service** (NHS). Since 1948 the NHS has looked after the health of everyone in Britain. Were your grandparents alive in 1948?

When he was a young boy, Jack Gooch walked 5 km to school each day.

'I had to walk to school no matter what the weather was like. I often got wet and cold in the winter, but the exercise kept me very fit.

'People do not walk as much as they used to. They go in cars and buses even for short trips. And they sit in front of the television at home a lot.

'When I was a child I lived a healthier life than many children today. Not everything is better than it used to be!'

7

COME IN, MRS SMITH

Do you know who this man is? He is a family doctor. He is waiting to see **patients** in his **surgery**. Can you see the computer behind him?

Most doctors work for the NHS. Patients do not pay money to go to see them. Have you been to the doctor recently?

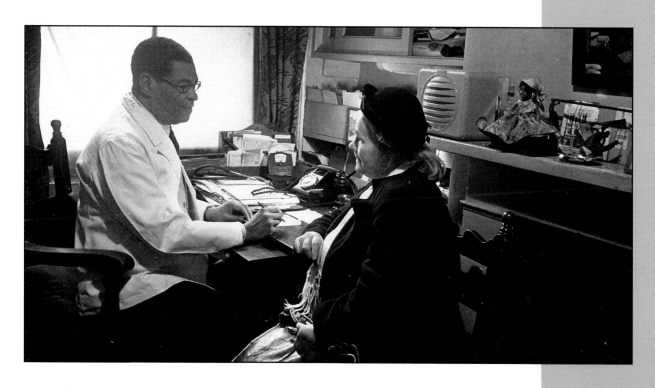

This woman is visiting her doctor in 1949. The doctor is finding out what is wrong with the woman. Then he will try to help her.

Look at the picture on the opposite page. What differences can you see between the two surgeries? Today doctors do not just try to make sick people better. They tell people how to lead healthier lives, so that they do not get ill so often.

This drawing of a doctor and a patient was done more than 150 years ago. Is the patient in hospital?

In those days doctors visited people in their homes. Everyone had to pay for the doctor to visit. Rich people were seen and treated but poor people usually did not have enough money.

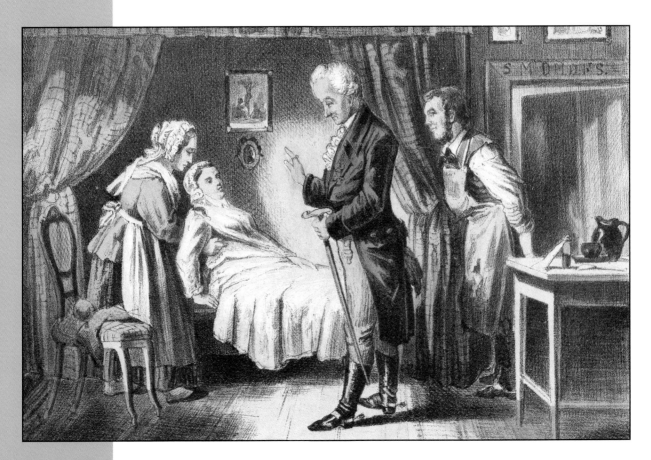

Janet Rigby was born in 1924. She remembers her dad telling her how worried he was about going to see the doctor in 1919.

'Here's my dad in hospital. He's the second person on the right of the picture.

'Dad was very ill but he did not go to the doctor for a long time. He was worried that it would cost too much.

'In the end, he did see the doctor. The doctor sent him to hospital. That cost even more money!'

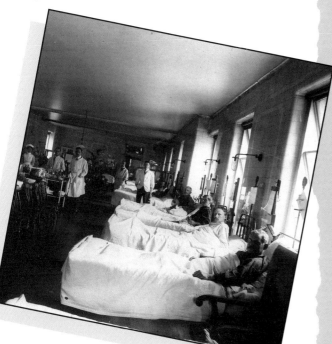

11

This girl is brushing her teeth. How often do you brush your teeth? Can you remember what happened the last time you went to the dentist?

Dentists check our teeth and gums to see if they are healthy. Nowadays, if dentists find a tooth with a hole they put a **filling** in it. Have you ever had a filling?

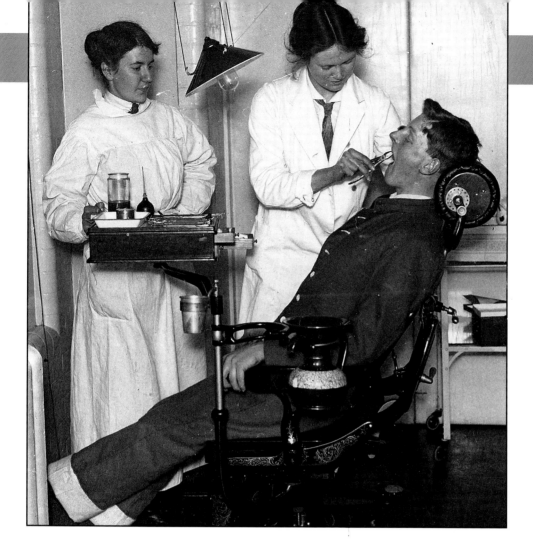

Here is a dentist at work in 1917. The treatment looks as if it hurts a lot, doesn't it?

At this time most people never visited a dentist. If there was something wrong with a tooth, it was usually pulled out. By the time they were forty, many people had no teeth left!

This is a hospital **operating theatre**, where patients go for **operations**.

Can you see the special machines in this picture? These machines help **surgeons** to perform very difficult operations. Nowadays doctors can give patients new hips, and even replace important parts of our bodies like hearts or lungs. These operations were not possible thirty years ago. Do you know someone who has had an operation?

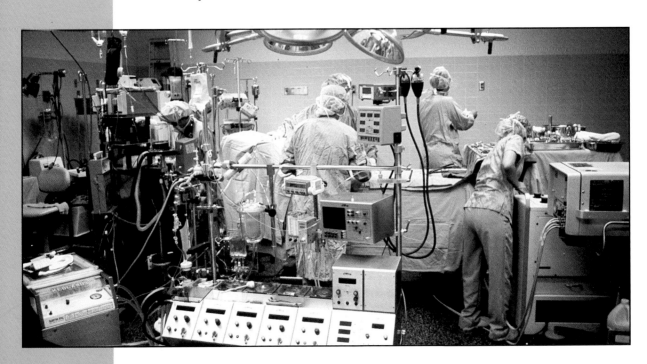

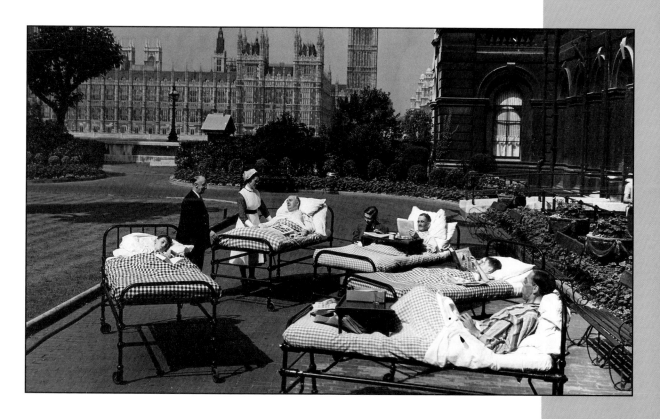

These patients have been moved out of a London hospital to spend the afternoon in the open air. Can you see the young boys?

The picture was taken in 1937. At that time it was usual for patients to stay in hospital for many weeks. Doctors did not have the medicines to make them better quickly. Staying in hospital for such a long time was very boring.

Look at this race. It is between children with **disabilities**. Do you know anyone who uses a wheelchair?

Nowadays people with disabilities can live very active lives. Modern wheelchairs are very light so they can be moved around easily. To help wheelchair users, many modern buildings have **ramps** as well as stairs.

A **physiotherapist** is helping this boy to walk. He has a metal support on his leg.

The picture was taken in 1947. The boy had been unable to walk for years. Now he has been taught new exercises so that he can walk. One hundred years earlier doctors would not have known how to help him. He would not have been able to move around at all.

In the past there were very few places where people with bad learning disabilities could be treated and looked after. Sometimes, if their families could not care for them, they were sent to places called **asylums**. The people in this picture are in an asylum.

This young man (on the right) with very bad learning disabilities is being taught how to cook for himself.

Today, people with very bad learning disabilities are taught how to look after themselves. We know much more about how to help them get the most out of life. There are many organizations that help them to set up their own homes.

Ow! This baby is having an **injection**. Do you think she is enjoying it?

Soon after they are born babies have injections against many diseases. In the last **century** thousands of babies died of diseases that can be easily stopped now.

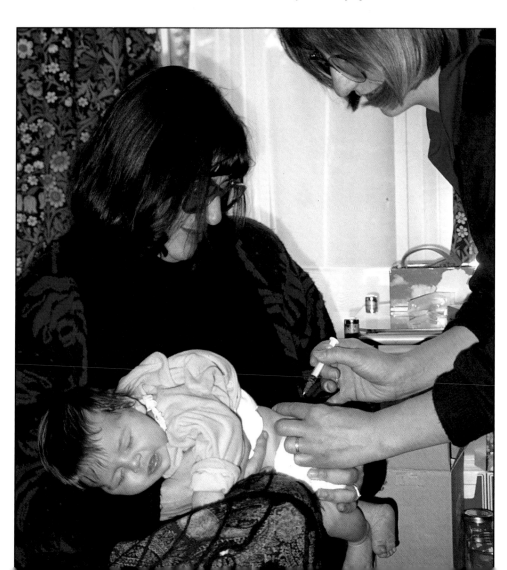

Do you like taking medicine? This baby is having special medicine to stop him getting a disease called polio. The picture was taken in 1961.

Polio used to kill many children. It left others unable to move parts of their bodies. Ask your grandparents if they remember the disease.

This is a chemist's shop in 1912. It sells medicines. What else can you buy from a chemist's shop?

Medicines have changed over the last seventy-five years. But some doctors find that medicines used long ago are still very useful. New ideas are not always better than old ones.

George Allen's father was a bus driver in the 1920s. George remembers his dad telling him about the **epidemic** of an illness called influenza (flu).

'I remember dad telling me about this photograph of him, taken in 1920.

'A terrible flu epidemic began in 1918, just after the **First World War**. Doctors tried all sorts of ways to stop the disease spreading. Thousands of people died, including my aunt.

'The photograph shows dad spraying the inside of his bus to kill the **germs**. It didn't do much good though.'

This new-born baby is ill. Doctors have put him in a special machine to help him get better. The machine keeps him warm. It also keeps out all germs.

Today there are machines and medicines just for sick babies. The baby in this picture will soon get better and be able to go home. Fifty years ago he would probably have died.

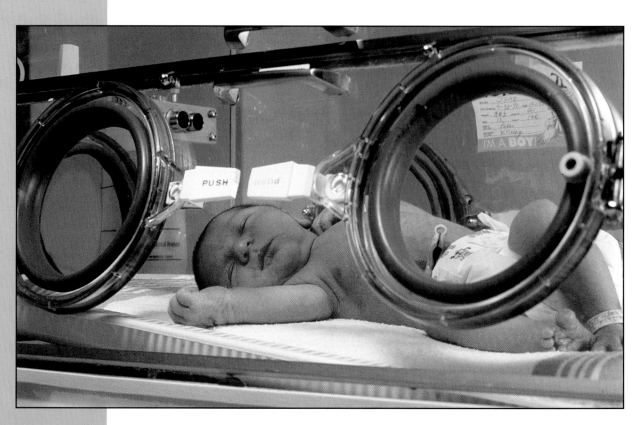

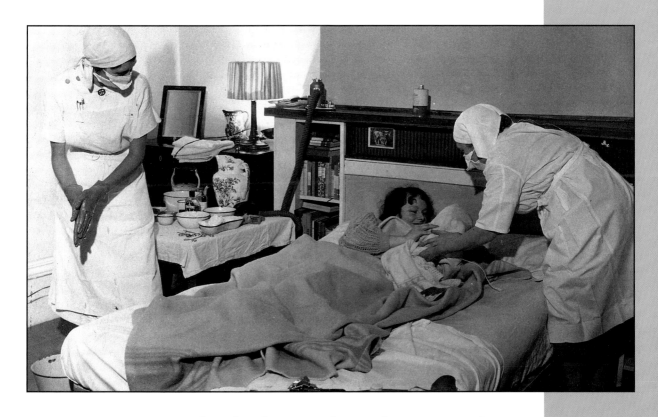

Can you see the baby in this photograph, taken in 1957? It is in the bundle of blankets near the mother. The baby has just been born at home. This was unusual even in the 1950s.

Before the **Second World War** babies were often born at home. Now most are born in hospital, where there are doctors to help. Do you know where you were born?

KEEPING FIT

These women are in an exercise class. Do you know anyone who goes to an exercise class? They are very popular. Doctors tell us to look after our health. They ask us to take lots of exercise and eat healthy food. This helps us not to get ill so often.

Can you read the writing on these posters? The photograph was taken during the Second World War. The woman is giving cigarettes to be sent to soldiers.

Fifty years ago doctors did not know that smoking was very bad for you. People smoked much more than they do today. Today, there are many public places where people are not allowed to smoke, such as trains, buses and cinemas. Do you think that this is a good idea?

This is a poster from the Second World War. It shows people how to stay healthy by eating the right food.

During the war the country was short of some foods, such as meat and sugar. People had to eat more fresh vegetables and salads instead. This helped them to stay healthy. Do you know what sorts of food are good for you?

David Farmer will never forget the PE classes he did in 1940.

'When I joined the army in 1940, over fifty years ago, we often played sport and did PE. It was hard work, but good fun.

'Doctors today are always going on about sport and exercise. They talk as if it is something new.

'I am at the front of this picture. I look pretty fit, don't I? Fitter than I am today!'

Talk to people

Ask grown-ups you know well about the changes they remember in people's health. The best person to talk to would be a doctor, a nurse or a dentist. You could ask them about medicines, treatments and hospitals, going to the doctor or dentist and keeping fit. Perhaps your grandparents remember the National Health Service (NHS) being set up?

Use your eyes

You can also learn about people's health in the past by looking at pictures and by reading books. The advertisements in old books, papers and magazines tell you about popular medicines. Look at pictures and read reports about changes taking place in health care (get an adult to help you).

Read all about it

These modern books are also useful:
Healthy Living series (Wayland, 1990)
My Book About The Body by Wayne Jackman (Wayland, 1991)

Making a display

Your class might enjoy making a display about people's health over the last seventy-five years. You could include things such as how long people lived, which were the most common diseases, how much medical treatment and medicines cost and how hospital treatments have changed.

GLOSSARY

Asylums   Places of safety.

Century   A period of a hundred years.

Disabilities   Having a particular part of the body that does not work properly.

Disease   Illness.

Epidemic   When a disease makes many people ill at the same time.

Filling   Something dentists put into a hole in a tooth to stop it going rotten.

First World War   The war which lasted from 1914 to 1918.

Germs   Tiny living things that can make people ill.

Injection   Putting medicine into a patient's body with a needle.

National Health Service (NHS)   The National Health Service was set up in 1948 to give free health care to everyone in Britain.

Operating theatre   The room in a hospital where operations take place.

Operations   When surgeons work on people's bodies to make them better.

Patients   People being treated by doctors or dentists.

Physiotherapist   Someone who helps patients get better with special exercises.

Ramps   Slopes that connect two levels.

Rickets   An illness which stops bones growing properly.

Second World War   The war which lasted from 1939 to 1945.

Surgeons   Doctors who perform operations.

Surgery   The place where a doctor or dentist sees patients.

INDEX